GW00568484

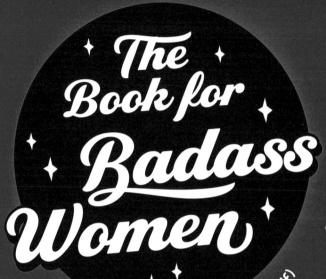

The Book for Badass Women

(Because the Patriarchy Won't Smash Itself)

Harriet Dyer

summersdale

THE BOOK FOR BADASS WOMEN

Text by Anna Lou Walker

An Hachette UK Company
www.hachette.co.uk

Summersdale Publishers Ltd
Part of Octopus Publishing Group Limited
Carmelite House
50 Victoria Embankment
LONDON
EC4Y 0DZ
UK

www.summersdale.com

Printed and bound in Poland

ISBN: 978-1-80007-193-3

Substantial discounts on bulk quantities of Summersdale books are available to corporations, professional associations and other organizations. For details contact general enquiries: telephone: +44 (0) 1243 771107 or email: enquiries@summersdale.com.

Contents

Do not live
someone else's life
and someone else's idea
of what womanhood is.
Womanhood is you.
Womanhood is everything
that's inside of you.

VIOLA DAVIS

Introduction

Badass women are something special. They're tough. They're fun. They take no shit and they do no harm. They lift other women up and never bring other women down. This little guide will show you how to fight for what you believe in and shake off the expectations of society. *The Book for Badass Women* is about challenging everything you've been taught about what it means to be a woman, including how to look and how to behave. Because learning to be a badass really means learning to be yourself.

Chapter 1

I Am Whoever I Say I Am

Badass women know who they are. Being a badass means having a rock-solid sense of self-belief – you need to *know* that you are hot shit. In this chapter, we'll question the ways you've been told you *should* be – how you should look, what you should wear, how you should act – and instead discover the ways that you *are*. Because the only person who gets to tell you how to be, is you!

Be you

You are the only person who can be you. So why waste your energy trying to be somebody else? Your individuality is your superpower and harnessing your uniqueness is the best thing you can do for yourself. Learning to live as authentically as possible will not only boost your confidence, but open doors for your career, social life and relationships. Thankfully there's no longer a single definition of how women should look, how they ought to think or what they should do – so run with it!

Stick it to them

Women are bombarded all day every day with messages about how we should and shouldn't act. Billboards featuring unrealistic representations of women, TV ads for diet shakes, lyrics that repeat the same tired stereotypes. All this messaging can be exhausting, and when you allow it to dictate your behaviour, it's easy to feel like you'll never measure up. Enough is enough. Give society's pressures the middle finger and start living your life exactly how *you* want. Measure yourself by nothing but your own expectations and you'll find a powerful sense of liberation.

All by yourself

"What's a queen without a king?" asks the caption of that smug Instagram couple who've been together *forever*. Well, historically speaking, the answer is "more powerful". At its best, a relationship is a source of mutual support and respect, but at its worst, it's a drain on your energy, time and happiness. We live in a society designed for couples, but if you are single take some time to be completely and utterly unattached and enjoy the magnificent power of being alone. By doing this, you'll gain confidence, independence and the clarity to know exactly what you want. That way, if you do choose to enter into a partnership, you'll still be able to remain true to yourself.

Be yourself. The world will adjust.

MANABI BANDYOPADHYAY

The power of "no"

What if there was a simple word that could help ease the pressures, stresses and inconveniences in your life? Well, there is, and it only has two letters – "NO!" This magnificent word is no longer the preserve of stubborn toddlers, and if used correctly, it has the power to transform your life. Women are conditioned by society to be affable and eager to please, which is also one of the ways it controls them. A lifetime of this conditioning can be hard to unlearn, but try taking "no" out for a day. Practise using it in low-stakes situations, such as turning down that after-work drink when you're feeling burned out, then break it out when you're next in a situation that makes you uncomfortable – like saying no to covering for an over-demanding colleague. Now sit back and observe the instant power points you gain.

If you were meant
to be controlled,
you'd have come
with a remote

Believe in yourself

Think about the people you've looked up to the most during your life, and you'll quickly realize they most likely have one thing in common – an unshakable sense of self-belief.

Before you can take on the world, you've got to take on your own self-doubts. Try writing down all the things stopping you from believing you're the bomb and tackle them one by one. Spend some time trying to rationalize your insecurities, and see if you can find any truth in them. You should quickly realize how baseless a lot of your worries are, so you can stop wasting time on self-doubt and start investing time in self-confidence!

I'VE ALWAYS DONE WHAT I WANT AND BEEN EXACTLY WHO I AM.

Billie Eilish

BE KIND TO YOURSELF

The way we talk to ourselves is fundamental in shaping how we feel. If you're always insulting yourself or questioning your abilities, you're not exactly going to feel on top of the world. Being a mean girl to yourself is a simple shortcut to feeling like crap. Instead, make a pact to begin treating yourself the way you would a close friend – with kindness, understanding and forgiveness – and you'll be well on the way to revolutionizing the way you feel about your life.

Take yourself on dates

As RuPaul once said, "If you can't love yourself, how in the hell are you gonna love somebody else?" When was the last time you spent an entire day doing whatever the heck you wanted? No catering for other people, no time sucked up in joyless chores, just 24 uninterrupted hours of treating yourself like a queen? If you can't remember, it's time to fix it.

Choose a day when you have no immediate responsibilities and plan a date just for yourself. Maybe go to see that movie you've been dying to watch but can't convince your friends to see. Or take a trip to your local gallery, stop for lunch on the way and be sure to relish not having to move at somebody else's pace. For inspiration, check out the fantastic TikTok star @holamiday. In her series, #HolaDares, she takes herself out to do the things many people are too afraid to do to show that they're really not as scary as you think, including solo activities such as going for dinner, to a club and even holidaying alone. If she can nail it, you know you can too.

The things that make us different, those are our superpowers.

Lena Waithe

Live life out loud

Louder for the people at the back! Now is the time to exist loudly and unapologetically. Don't be afraid to let people know exactly who you are – speak out about the things you like, shout about the things you don't. Laugh until you can't breathe and ugly cry when you need to. No longer are women seen and not heard – we're better when we're in full colour and heard shouting from the rooftops, so get out there and use your voice in every way you can.

Once you learn your value, you'll stop giving people discounts

Dress to express

Reclaim ownership of your body by making a promise to yourself to dress however the hell you want. Your favourite outfit is no longer on-trend? Who cares! Feel "too big" or "too skinny" to rock that dress you love? Say "Screw you" to those expectations and *wear the damn dress anyway!* It's your body and your rules. Dye your hair, get a tattoo, pierce your nose, wear clashing colours – throw the fashion rule book away and write your own. Dress yourself in whatever makes you feel good, whether that's towering heels or a scruffy pair of Converse. Don't worry about what other people think – refuse to tone yourself down to please somebody else. Learn to dress for yourself and not the opinions of others. It's time to put the fun back into your wardrobe.

*Above all, be
the heroine
of your life,
not the victim.*

NORA EPHRON

Practise body neutrality

If you find self-confidence challenging, the "body positivity movement" that has dominated Instagram feeds over the past few years might leave you feeling, well, body negative. Some women find the pressure to feel confident about their appearance actually just feels like another hurdle to overcome. If that's how you feel, forget body positivity and instead embrace "body neutrality". This focuses on acceptance rather than the overt celebration of your body. You don't have to love your body, but you definitely don't need to hate it. Let go of the pressures to perform and just let yourself *be*.

Kill your inner saboteur

It's dangerously easy to accept the authority of that strong voice in your head, but try to remember that inner voice isn't always *you* – often it's plain old internalized misogyny. Sometimes your inner voice is *actively* trying to make you doubt yourself, shame yourself or just generally make you feel like crap. But this isn't an epic David Attenborough voice-over – that inner voice doesn't always speak the truth. So next time your inner voice tells you something negative, call it out! Why is that the case? Where's the proof? And why couldn't the opposite be true? Get into the habit of questioning that nasty inner narrative, and you'll soon find the voice gets a lot quieter.

YOU'RE NUMBER ONE

People-pleasing is a difficult habit to unlearn, particularly in a society that constantly reminds women this is expected of them. But while pleasing other people can often be a kind and thoughtful thing to do, if you find you're neglecting your own needs, then the balance is all wrong.

Constantly sacrificing your happiness for somebody else's isn't OK. You may want to make the world a happier place, but that should never come at the cost of your own well-being. You are the most important person in your life, so start acting like it!

We should stop defining each other by what we are not and start defining ourselves by who we are.

EMMA WATSON

You are enough

Do yourself a favour. Find your nearest mirror, look yourself square in the eye and say these words: "I am enough." Now repeat them again. And again. Let it become a daily mantra. They may sound simple, but these three words have the power to revolutionize your life if you'd only let yourself truly hear them. You. Are. Enough. You're not *almost* enough. You don't have to wait until you get that promotion, learn to drive, lose weight or gain a cooler circle of friends – you *are* enough, exactly as you are. You are worthy of happiness and love.

No matter what adventures life may take you on, no matter how much your choices, priorities or styles may shift, this will never change – and there's so much freedom in that. Knowing that you're already enough just by being yourself gives you the permission and liberation to grow, make mistakes, try new things and fail *hard*. Because none of it takes away from your essential value and worthiness as a loved and deserving human being. Follow your aspirations wherever they may take you and know there is no need to prove yourself good enough. You already are, just by being you.

Forget the haters

The less you give a damn about what the world thinks of you, the more unsolicited opinions you're likely to provoke. Sadly, part and parcel of being your absolute authentic self is the burden of worrying about other people having thoughts about how you behave and the choices you make. Part of being a badass woman is learning to shrug off the negativity and to give the opinions of others zero power over your mood. It's a skill, and it takes practice, but the more you decide not to let the opinions of others take root in your mind, the freer you'll become.

EMBRACE
WHAT MAKES
YOU UNIQUE,
EVEN IF IT
MAKES OTHERS
UNCOMFORTABLE.

Janelle Monáe

Be *your* *own* cheerleader

Give me a "Y", give me an "O", give me a "U" – that's right, "YOU", the person you should always be cheering for. When you have nobody else in your corner, you'll always be able to count on one person to show up and hype you up – and that's yourself. That's why it's so important to treat yourself with kindness and believe in your vision with all you've got because at the end of the day, you are the only person you can rely on to *always* be in your corner.

YOU
ARE A
FORCE OF
NATURE

Sing yourself confident

For those days when you wake up feeling distinctly wallflower-esque, this powerhouse playlist will pull you up, dust off your shoulders and get you striding tall. Scan the QR code, put on your favourite outfit, pump up the volume and shake it off in style.

"Confident" by Demi Lovato
"Love Myself" by Hailee Steinfeld
"Titanium" by David Guetta (ft. Sia)
"Stronger (What Doesn't Kill You)" by Kelly Clarkson
"Brave" by Sara Bareilles
"Run the World (Girls)" by Beyoncé
"Juice" by Lizzo
"Shake It Off" by Taylor Swift
"Born This Way" by Lady Gaga
"Don't Stop Me Now" by Queen

A woman with a voice is, by definition, a strong woman.

Melinda Gates

ROLE MODEL ROLL CALL

As the saying goes, "You can't be what you can't see." Got dreams, but don't know any women who have achieved them? Then seek out role models who are living lives, working careers or making moves in the ways that you would like to. Read their biography, follow them on Instagram, shoot them a message on LinkedIn. You don't have to keep track of their every move, but keeping an eye on the women who have walked before you will help you to better see yourself in their shoes.

Collect your compliments

If you're struggling to see the good in yourself, try this simple exercise. For the next few weeks, every time somebody gives you a compliment, write it down on your phone or a piece of paper. Perhaps your hairstyling slayed this week, you bossed a presentation or you simply made a co-worker a killer cup of tea. No compliment is too small! Keep a note of it all and at the end of the week revisit your list for an instant confidence boost. You're doing so much better than you think. And if all the compliments make you feel better, pass it on! Paying a small compliment to someone could make their day.

Good vibe tribe

The people you choose to spend your time with have an enormous impact on who you are as a person – from your dirty sense of humour, to the songs that get you on the dancefloor, to your choice of career. Our friends and peers have the power to make us feel on top of the world or like the gum stuck to someone's shoe. It's important to remember your friends are your *chosen* family and that means you can *stop* choosing them when they no longer impact your life positively. If you have a friend who constantly belittles you, drains your energy or gets you into shady situations, don't feel obliged to continue spending time with them. Bad vibes are contagious, and the more time you spend with them, the more you'll find yourself mirroring their behaviour and attitudes, whether you mean to or not. Put your own needs first and distance yourself from anybody who doesn't make you feel great about yourself at all times. You're not being a bad friend – you're taking control of the person you're becoming.

Instead, choose to surround yourself with people who lift you up, support your ambitions and bring out the best in you – after all, your friends should be your biggest hype team.

You don't owe
prettiness to anyone.
Prettiness is not a rent
you pay for occupying a
space marked "female".

ERIN McKEAN

Nourish to flourish

There's no use working towards loving yourself if the food you're eating is making you feel rubbish, or you're surviving on a few snatched hours of sleep a night. To really work on building yourself up means caring for your body as well as your mind. Try to eat fruit and vegetables as often as you can, get some fresh air every day, take time to wind down before bed and get a full night's sleep rather than wasting the evening scrolling through social media. Self-care isn't selfish – it's vital for waking up with the fight and drive of a badass woman.

The question isn't who is going to let me – it's who is going to stop me.

AYN RAND

Everyday superpowers

Want to know a secret? Everyone is good at something. Isn't that exciting? It could be a hobby or a skill, like baking or tennis. Maybe it's something in your personality, such as being able to keep a cool head in a crisis or really listening to your friends. It could even be something small, like always remembering people's birthdays, making perfect playlists or knowing all the best swear words in French. Whatever your many and varied talents, be sure to cherish and nurture them. Celebrate your skills and be proud of what you can do. It's what makes you irreplaceable.

Chapter 2
Fight Like a Girl

Badass women aren't afraid to stand up for themselves and what they believe in. Going against society's expectations can be daunting, but it's the only way to feel truly empowered and authentic. This chapter is full of tips for defying the "rules" of womanhood and stepping into your true self.

ASK FOR
WHAT YOU WANT

Don't ask, don't get. So simple, but so true. Bashfulness won't get you anywhere in life, and it's scary to think how many women miss out on opportunities because they're simply too afraid to ask directly for what they want. Next time you find yourself in a situation where you want something specific, and you're in a position to have a conversation that could make it a reality, HAVE IT! Sure, it's scary sometimes, but ask yourself what's the worst thing that could happen and then *do it anyway*. You only have one life so don't live it timidly.

Give up being likeable

How many times a week do you stop to question whether your actions are likeable? From the way we ask for favours, to the way we speak to friends and family, to the punctuation we use in emails, women are constantly under pressure to do the *likeable* thing and prioritize people's opinions of us above all else. Here's a secret for you – this is *total bullshit,* and it's deliberate. If women are making sure they're liked, they've got less time for taking on the world. Once you give up trying to do the likeable thing and start doing what's right for you, nothing can stop you. The ironic thing? People will probably like you more for being authentic anyway!

Take up space

From our earliest days, women are trained to take up as little space as possible. Whether that's by being "seen and not heard", through aggressive weight loss marketing or because of the constant pressure to not "rock the boat". The result is that many of us go through life as a reduced version of ourselves. In adhering to this pressure to be *less*, you are agreeing to live a life in which you never express your fullest self. What a load of crap. The next time you feel the urge to move out of the way of a man striding down the street, to stay quiet in that meeting or to fold yourself up neatly when sat next to a manspreader, do the exact opposite. Take up every bit of the space you need in that moment and then some. You'll soon realize just how much of yourself you were holding back.

I'm tough,
I'm ambitious,
and I know exactly
what I want.
If that makes
me a bitch, OK.

MADONNA

Lions need to roar

Anger is a part of the human experience and feeling it is not a "bad" thing. Sometimes anger can be the right response to a situation — possibly even the healthiest one! So, if something has royally pissed you off, don't try to suppress it. Talk to somebody about how you're feeling and confront the root of what's bugging you. Scream into a pillow or aggressively play *Call of Duty*. It's OK to cry, and it's OK to feel angry. Allow yourself to express your anger in a healthy, safe place and that way you won't bring it with you when you need to get back to business.

What doesn't kill me had better run

My body, my rules

Nobody gets to tell you what to do with your body except you – and if they try? Fight back. No government, friend, employer or man has any business discussing what you do or don't do with your body because it belongs to you and absolutely nobody else. Want to grow your armpit hair? Slay. Enjoy your soft belly and fuller hips? Don't let anybody tell you to shrink them. And if somebody tries to tell you any different, don't be afraid to give them hell.

Run away
from men
who can't
handle your
ambition.

Reese Witherspoon

Never shrink yourself for somebody else

We've all been there. You meet someone who excites you and before you know it, you're contorting your entire being to try to become their ideal partner or friend. Whether that's changing your clothes, hairstyle or friends, remember this – sooner or later your old self will catch up and, when she does, she'll slap the hell out of you for trying to be someone you're not! Because when the right people come into your life, they'll want every bit of you just as you are. No compromises and no adjustments.

Speak your mind

We live in a world where women still have to shout to be heard, so it's time to warm up those vocal pipes. But being badass and loud isn't something that comes naturally to everyone. Some of us need serious practice to shout about who we are. If you're naturally soft-spoken, here are some tips for making yourself heard:

1. **Stand like a boss.** Posture speaks for us before we've even opened our mouths. When standing, keep your head high and pull your shoulders back. When sitting, keep your back straight and lean forwards slightly, as if leaning into the conversation.

2. **Project!** Learning projection techniques can help to ensure your voice carries further. Before you speak, relax your tummy, inhale quickly and then let out a slow exhale, keeping your upper body as still as possible. When you start to speak, inhale deeply at the end of each sentence before you start your next one as this will help keep your projection going.

3. **Slow down.** There's no point in being un-apologetically loud if nobody can tell what you're saying. If you're feeling nervous, chances are you're talking too fast, so take a breath, adjust your pace and make sure the room understands exactly what you came to say.

Girls are told they have to
be a princess and fragile.
It's bullshit. I identify
more with being a
warrior, a fighter.

EMMA WATSON

SET BOUNDARIES

Here's a secret — you have the power and right to tell people exactly how to treat you. Setting clear, verbal boundaries with the people in your life, be they colleagues, friends, family or romantic partners, is crucial not only for protecting your well-being but also for helping those relationships to flourish. Boundaries will vary from person to person, but key questions to ask yourself are: how does this relationship make me feel? How can this relationship bring the most positive energy to my life? Do I feel able to communicate honestly with this person? Anyone worth their salt will respect your boundaries.

DO NO HARM: TAKE NO SHIT

Be the star of your show

Visualize your favourite movie. Would you enjoy it as much if the main character constantly acted according to the whims of a minor side character instead of their own desires? Then why are you not acting like the main character in your own damn life? Living your life according to the expectations of others means you are living half a life. To reaffirm your role as the star of your story, spend a day romancing yourself. Buy fresh flowers, take yourself for lunch or coffee and treat yourself with the gentle romance of a main character. Reminding yourself of your worth will soon translate to making decisions that reflect your value.

Life's a bitch. You've got to go out and kick ass.

Maya Angelou

Learn when to sashay away

Badass women know when it's time to walk away. Whether it's a relationship or a work project, there's one simple rule that will tell you when it's time to say "no": ask yourself – is it making you feel bad more than it's making you feel good? If the answer is yes, then life is too short for that shit. Any person or project that makes you feel bad, pressured, insecure or any negative emotion is dragging you down, and you will never be the best version of yourself while contaminated by that energy. Learning when to walk away from toxicity is crucial for living a life where you're truly in the driver's seat.

Practise radical honesty

Time to get brutal. Practising radical honesty is a liberating experience, particularly for women who are conditioned since childhood to soften every exchange (smiley emojis, we're looking at you). Set yourself the challenge of getting through a day expressing your thoughts exactly how they manifest and enjoy the euphoria of being utterly authentic. This doesn't mean you need to slag off your friend's new boyfriend, it just means being more honest with yourself and your needs, and not being afraid to say when enough is enough.

Don't play the game – change the game

Dump their ass

Find yourself awake long into the night pondering the same question or chatting your girlfriends' ears off over lunch with the same query: "Should I dump my partner?" The answer, I'm afraid, is always an unequivocal "yes". Why are you wasting your time and energy in a situation that doesn't bring positivity to your life? If your romantic partner is making you feel bad more than they are making you feel like the living, breathing goddess that you are, it's time to rid yourself of that dead weight. You'll be walking taller in no time.

THERE'S NOTHING A MAN CAN DO, THAT I CAN'T DO BETTER AND IN HEELS.

Ginger Rogers

Shut down sexists

We all know the feeling. You're at a party having a great time when someone feels the need to butt into your conversation and casually make a remark so sexist it makes your blood boil, despite the ice in your drink. "It was just a joke," they guffaw when your stony face makes it clear you're not prepared to laugh along. Moments like this can be intimidating, but learning to speak up when somebody makes sexist remarks is extremely empowering.

Try these phrases for an effective shut down:

"Can you explain what you mean by that?" Often just the process of having to break down a sexist comment is enough to make someone feel embarrassed and think twice before making a remark next time.

"What? Can you repeat that?" Pretend you didn't hear their comment and keep asking them to repeat their stupidity until they get the message.

"Doesn't it have to be funny to be a joke?" Sometimes a sassy response is the fastest way to turn the tables on someone who is trying to dominate the conversation.

NOTE: Always ensure your safety! If anybody's comments are making you feel unsafe, leave the situation as soon as you can.

You are resilient as hell

Women are some of the most resilient creatures on the planet. Look around you at the women you love and think about the collective struggles you have endured together – aren't we remarkable? Take strength from the collective resilience of the women in your life as a reminder that you are capable of getting through anything this world might throw at you. And if you can't? Then you're capable of bouncing back, better than before.

The odds might seem insurmountable now, but you are made of stronger stuff than your challenges. Remember, nothing in life lasts forever, especially not feelings of being overwhelmed. If all else fails, try the 333 method. Will you care about this problem in three hours? Three days? Three years? The answer is almost always no, which means a better tomorrow is already on its way.

We're here now, women are in the world, and we will not be bullied.

MERYL STREEP

Study the art of sass

Ah, the specific hell of overthinking during a post-confrontation shower, when you find your brain has no problem crafting the exact comeback that would have shut down your aggravator and seen you leave the scenario triumphant. If you find yourself constantly frustrated that the right words only come to you *after* a disagreement, you're in luck. Perfecting in-the-moment sass is a skill just like any other – and it comes with practice. Next time somebody rubs you up the wrong way or tries to palm off a task you know isn't your responsibility, just say something. Anything. You may not start out with winning witty shutdowns, but with time, you'll find your brain catches up to your gut, and you're expressing yourself way before that post-shower clarity hits.

EXIST ON YOUR OWN DAMN TERMS

Be your own best friend

If you wouldn't say it to your best friend, why the hell are you saying it to yourself? When things fall apart, criticizing yourself will only make the situation worse. It won't make things better, *and* it could rid you of the motivation to carry on. Instead, speak to yourself as you would a close friend and encourage yourself to see the situation from a more positive perspective. Tell yourself, for example, that you haven't failed; it just hasn't worked out this time. Don't be afraid to give yourself another chance. With a little kindness and self-respect, you'll get there next time.

We can't be feminine
and be feminists?
I want to be a fucking
feminist and wear a
fucking Peter Pan collar.
So fucking what?

ZOOEY DESCHANEL

Haters gonna hate

Behind every successful woman is an internet troll telling her she shouldn't have bothered. The world can be a cruel place and, sadly, negative voices tend to follow success. In our constantly connected age, these voices are louder than ever. Whether it's work frenemies gossiping about your new position or comments from strangers on your social media, it's time to hit the block button, both real and imaginary. Don't let other people stand in the way of your vision or let their negative views cloud your positivity. After all, the sun continues shining, no matter how many clouds try to block her out.

Stay in control of sex

Have you ever let fear of "ruining the moment" in the bedroom stop you from asking for what you really want? Stop that shit right now. Try to train yourself to prioritize your security and satisfaction over the perceptions of your sexual partner. Set clear boundaries and make sure that your partner sticks to them. If they don't, don't engage in sexual activity with them.

Want to use condoms? Any response that's not an enthusiastic "of course" is a red flag. Not happy exploring a certain kink? Then it's off the table. The more you advocate for the kind of sex you really want, the less you'll find yourself involved with partners who aren't willing to make you feel absolutely safe, secure and satisfied!

Check your reflection

The moments in life when you learn the most about yourself are almost always spent alone. Those long morning walks you took when you were trying to decide whether to drop out of college. The night you rode the bus all the way home after New Year's Eve and reflected on the year you'd had. The time you opened a results letter all alone and felt a world of new possibilities course through your veins. Creating intentional moments for reflection is a great way to take control of your life. Think about the moments where you've had breakthroughs and try to intentionally bring them about. Always get your best ideas while walking? Take more walks. Return from long drives with it all figured out? Go out of your way to drive somewhere scenic. Life moves fast, so make sure you're making time to take it in before it passes you by.

To harness this power even further, try journaling. Take a notebook and pen with you the next time you undertake a moment of reflection and write down how you feel. Nothing coming to you? Try free writing – just note down exactly what thoughts enter your mind; it doesn't matter if they make sense or not. Eventually, you'll find your most pressing concerns float to the surface. You might just be surprised by what you find.

I do not belong to anyone but myself. And neither do you.

Ariana Grande

Take a self-defence class

Stopping street harassment and assault is not the job of women; it's the responsibility of men. But taking a self-defence class is still a good idea and will make you feel more secure and in control when walking home late at night. Not only will it offer you a sense of security, but self-defence classes are great for self-confidence, showing you just how much power you're capable of unleashing, should you set your mind to it. Take some friends and turn the evening into an event. Who knows, you might just unearth a hidden talent!

Explore beyond the binary

As a society, we're questioning the role of gender in our lives more than ever and taking stock of your own gender presentation can be extremely liberating. You might be surprised to discover how much of your personality or expression is informed by your identity as a "woman" rather than the truth of how you'd like to act, dress or live your life.

Put aside a moment to take stock of your life and question those elements that are performing to an idea of what a girl *should* or *shouldn't* do – and then question them. Partaking in activities, behaviours or styles traditionally labelled as masculine doesn't make you any less of a woman – and even if they did, who cares? Enjoy getting to the root of whoever *you* are, because you exist beyond the boundaries of any label.

Chapter 3

She Believed She Could, So She Did

Badass women are driven. They have big ambitions and big plans to help get them there. Drown out the haters by focusing on your vision and creating a road map to the top. This chapter will help you to go after your goals and define the life that you want for yourself.

Learn how to fail

"Learning how to fail is actually learning how to succeed better," says journalist and author Elizabeth Day, host of the successful *How to Fail* podcast in which she asks celebrities about the three failures that have shaped their lives. It's an empowering listen that advocates the importance of failing to truly learn who you are and shape the life you want to lead.

Set yourself the challenge of writing down your own three biggest failures and note down the positive ways in which they have changed your life – even if it was to make you certain you never wanted to fail in that way again. You'll soon start to see future failures as the groundwork for future success.

Set and manifest

All badass women have one thing in common — vision. To set about achieving your goals, you need to have a clear idea of what they are. You can't find the route to your destination without first knowing where the hell you're going. Write a different goal at the top of a few sheets of paper. Then think about your desired time frame and the steps you'll need to get there. Creating a road map to success will give you the structure you need to take actionable steps. When ambitions become tangible plans, you will be far more likely to head in the right direction.

Feminism means choice

A key goal of feminism is the fight for equality of choice and opportunity. Feminism isn't setting out to say that certain choices are "unfeminist". You can be a feminist and wear makeup. You can be a feminist and be a housewife. You can be a feminist and take your spouse's last name. For centuries, women have fought for your right to *choose*. That's where true emancipation lies! Honour your feminist foremothers by living your life in the most authentic way possible, whatever that means for you.

"Why the fuck not me" should be your motto.

Mindy Kaling

Pressure makes diamonds

Pressure makes diamonds. Remind yourself of that the next time you find yourself in hot water, and it may transpire that being thrown to the wolves sees you return leading the pack. So, when you find yourself in a stressful situation, whether at work, home or with friends, don't let it set you spiralling. Instead, remain grounded.

Tell yourself, "I can" – say it aloud to confirm it – and let any doubting thoughts merely drift through your head and back out again without allowing them to take root. Focus instead on what is in front of you now as this will help you to keep control of your emotions, maintain a clear head and begin laying out your plan, so you can deal with the situation calmly and confidently. Now that's badass.

Be the CEO they said you should marry

Dream big

"Some women choose to follow men and some women choose to follow their dreams. If you're wondering which way to go, remember that your career will never wake up and tell you that it doesn't love you anymore." If it's a mantra good enough for Lady Gaga, it's good enough for us.

It's essential not to pin your happiness on other people in your life, whether that is family, friends or a partner. You need to find more dependable reasons to get up and go in the morning, pushed by your passions and purpose. This might be a career or a hobby. Maybe it's your morning runs and your dream of completing a marathon. Maybe it's your new love for knitting and your goal to craft the world's biggest poncho. Whatever it is, place your dreams at the centre of your universe.

I DON'T LIKE TO GAMBLE, BUT IF THERE'S ONE THING I'M WILLING TO BET ON, IT'S MYSELF.

Beyoncé

Celebrate the little things

One of the worst parts of becoming an adult is realising there are no longer gold stars for a small job well done – so it's time to make your own! To inject more joy and satisfaction into your life, don't forget to celebrate the small milestones. Sent that email you've been putting off for weeks? Hero. Took the risk with that bold new hair colour? You're a legend. Finally remembered to put the bins out? Nailed it! Taking time to celebrate the little things is a great way to check in and remind yourself you're doing pretty damn well.

Never break the chain

Did you know that in the US there are more CEOs named John in the leading 500 firms than there are women? It's time to harness the power of the chain to break that. What's the chain? It's a powerful attitude to your career that sees you look up to the women who came before you and reach back to pull up other women when you succeed.

Think about your dream job, then use tools such as LinkedIn to find women who have already got there. Note the rungs on the ladder that helped them reach the top spot. This will present you with a clear road map to your goals. You may even be surprised by some of their career histories. Not every success story looks the same, and all experience can be useful, given the right attitude.

Want to take your ambition a step further? Reach out to one of these women, tell them why you admire them, a little about your own aspirations and then ask if they have the time to meet for a coffee or to answer some of your questions about your dream job. Just remember to return the favour once it's you in the covetable hot seat. Badass women always pull other women up; they don't tread on the toes of those behind them.

They'll tell you
you're too loud, that you
need to wait your turn
and ask for permission.
Do it anyway.

ALEXANDRIA OCASIO-CORTEZ

Remember why you started

Early on in your career journey, create a vision board. This visual reference point should contain everything that inspires you about your ambition. What you love about it, what you want to achieve from it and how thinking about it makes you feel. You can do this on the computer, but even better, grab a glue stick, some old magazines and felt tips and do it by hand. Create a colourful poster that sums up everything you think of when you dream of your career future. This way, when things get tough, something goes wrong, or you lose sight of the purpose behind those long nights and early morning commutes, you can look back at your vision board and see in an instant what makes it all worthwhile.

DUST SETTLES; I DON'T

Ask for help

There are no bonus points for succeeding on your own. Behind every successful woman is an army of other successful women, giving her advice, supporting her with her workload or holding her hair back after too many tequilas at the office party. Don't be afraid to ask for help – in fact, make a habit of it. We are all surrounded by countless badass women whose opinions, outlooks and knowledge can add so much value to our lives and our perspectives. Get listening!

Far too many
people are looking
for the right person,
instead of trying to
be the right person.

GLORIA STEINEM

FOCUS ON YOU

All competitive runners will tell you that looking over your shoulder to check in on the competition is a sure way to lose out on first place. The second an athlete turns their head, they've stopped running to win – they're running to avoid losing. And this isn't only true for athletes. If you spend your life in the cycle of comparison, measuring your worth, your progress and your achievements by comparing them to those of others, it will only result in you no longer living for yourself. So, keep your eyes on the prize. Stop looking back and start looking forward, because you're a winner, baby.

Trust your gut

A woman's instincts are an enormously powerful thing. How many times have you felt in your gut that something was off, only to ignore it and later have your gut proven right? Women's intuition may be treated as something of a joke, but there's science behind it too.

Experts claim that it's women's heightened ability to read facial expressions and body language that gives us the edge when it comes to our gut. Go with it. That little voice in the pit of your stomach almost always knows the right thing to do, so trust her.

PROVE THEM WRONG

It's never too late

The average age for women to give up on their dream job is 30, and yet there are countless women in the public eye who have proved that age really ain't nothing but a number when it comes to chasing your dreams.

Director Ava DuVernay never went to film school and didn't pick up a camera until she was 32. Ten years later, she had an Oscar nomination. Actress Jessica Chastain only had her first movie credit aged 30. Iconic designer Vivienne Westwood's first catwalk show wasn't until she was 40. All this to say, it's never too late, and you'll get to where you're meant to be in the end. And if you're still not there? Then it's not the end.

Bitches get stuff done.

Tina Fey

Be suspicious of social media

When your mama told you, "comparison is the thief of joy", she wasn't lying. And living in the social media age has us more glued to the cycle of comparison than ever before, thanks to the daily intrusion of Instagram, Twitter and TikTok in our lives.

Find yourself looking at your phone first thing in the morning, last thing at night, on every bus journey and toilet break? Then comparison is probably already affecting you more than you think. The messages we feed into our brains through our screen time are powerful things, and while a lot of this can be positive, it is irresponsible not to realize the damage it can be causing you too.

It's time for a long-overdue cull of that follow list. Take the time to look through your social profiles and unfollow any accounts that don't bring you joy. Particularly anybody you follow purely through lifestyle or body envy. Then take an honest look at your screen time. Clocking up endless hours on TikTok or Instagram isn't doing you any good. Experts say that, outside of work, any more than two hours of screen time is doing us damage by losing us sleep, straining our eyes and fuelling addictive behaviours. Time to pull the plug.

Fake it 'til you make it

If you spend your time in the shower deeply immersed in giving the greatest Academy Award acceptance speeches of all time, then it's time to harness those acting skills for good, and put the well-worn phrase "fake it 'til you make it" to the test. Thoughts have the power to become feelings, so if you're feeling shy, scared, sad or unsure, try pretending to yourself and others that you're the very picture of certainty, confidence and calm. Fake it for long enough and those active thoughts will melt into your real feelings.

Another world is
not only possible,
she is on her way.
On a quiet day,
I can hear her
breathing.

ARUNDHATI ROY

It's a stumble, not a fall

Spoiler alert – things are going to go wrong. Part of life is learning that the road to every goal comes with some major speed bumps along the way, but don't be discouraged when things get tough. Maybe reaching a goal is more difficult than you anticipated. Perhaps it's taking longer than you expected to see results from some hard work. But the best things in life never come without you having to break a sweat.

If you're finding things difficult, that probably means you're right on track. At times like this, cast your mind back to what made you start out in the first place. Refresh your sense of motivation by retracing your steps to that first spark of determination to give yourself the kick up the bum you need to hype yourself up and keep going.

HAVE YOUR OWN BACK

IT'S NEVER TOO LATE TO START AGAIN

Have you ever tried to make a project work so hard that you've stormed through three of your best notepads, hours of screen time and all the best swear words you know? If you've been working towards a goal for a long time, you might feel duty-bound to continue, but sometimes there's nothing more powerful than a fresh start.

Whatever stage you're at, whether you've been working on your project for five days or five years, you can always change the direction if it's no longer serving you. Your time is precious, so don't waste it on something you're not passionate about.

Around the world...
women are rising,
taking leadership,
taking their destiny
into their own hands,
inspiring all of us.

ANGELINA JOLIE

You gotta have faith

The key to appearing confident is surprisingly simple – you've got to believe in your own sauce! If you don't have faith in yourself and your convictions, then how the hell do you expect anybody else to? Trust your ideas and opinions and share them confidently – you've got this!

If you're presenting a topic publicly at an interview, meeting or in a presentation, then remember to speak slowly and calmly, make eye contact and speak from the heart. When you take the time to let your passion and belief in your ideas come through, there'll be no stopping your shine.

Stop procrastinating!

Want a sure-fire way to feel like a bad bitch with minimal effort? Write a list of all the annoying little tasks that have been on your to-do list for weeks, set a timer for 20 minutes and complete as many of them as you can.

When the timer's up, you'll have a sense of achievement and relieve the stress that the constantly growing to-do list in the background was causing you. Procrastinating, even over something small, is an easy way to make yourself feel bad, but facilitate that 20-minute spot every day or two, and you'll soon start to feel on top of your shit.

Learn to rest, not give up

"You have as many hours in the day as Beyoncé", reads the tweet that's had you staring into the void for the past 20 minutes. There's so much pressure on modern women to "have it all" that it's easy to find yourself spiralling trying to juggle the demands of a satisfying work, social and love life. But these peppy phrases spun out for likes and retweets are never quite what they seem.

For one thing, Beyoncé has managed to "buy" herself extra hours in her day through her wealth and numerous staff! It would be immeasurably easier to achieve all your goals if you too had a "glam squad" and a team of committed helpers by your side at all times. But you are not Beyoncé, and you don't have to be on your A-game all the time. Allow yourself to switch off and give yourself room to rest. A day spent doing nothing is not a day wasted; it's a day spent nourishing your soul, so that you can come back stronger than ever.

Being a badass doesn't mean being forever on the go, achieving endless wins with zero downtime between kicking butt and living the dream. It actually means recognizing your needs and taking them seriously. Cut yourself some slack!

IF THEY DON'T GIVE YOU A SEAT AT THE TABLE BRING A FOLDING CHAIR.

Shirley Chisholm

Dare to dream

There's a time and a place for realism. No, you probably aren't going to marry Brad Pitt or fly to Mars. But when it comes to your ambitions, don't be afraid to go after something that doesn't seem likely right now.

Remember that every expert, professional or master of their field was once a beginner who knew nothing. We all have to start somewhere, and it's when we try new things that we experience the most growth. If you have a vision, push yourself out of your comfort zone to try and make it happen. You never know where it might lead or what new opportunities will open up for you.

Don't fear the fire – become it

Motivate yourself

Sometimes the difference between making your dreams come true and leaving them as figments of your imagination comes down to self-belief. This sounds like a small thing, but it's far from it. Self-belief is what motivates you to get started, and it's what will keep you going through the tougher times ahead. If you're starting out, try setting a small goal first to prove to yourself that you're capable – write 500 words of that novel or run a mile of that marathon. Small acts add up, and you'll soon find you're well on your way to your goal before you know it.

Chapter 4

Empowered Women Empower Women

Badass women lift up other women, and this chapter is all about the importance of empowering other women. Calling on their help when you need it and offering your own support in return. After all, behind every good woman is a badass girl gang.

Be generous with compliments

A well-placed compliment has the power to transform someone's day – and you can pay one any time you like! Set yourself a goal of complimenting at least one woman every day. And here's an extra challenge, don't let more than three of those seven compliments be about their appearance. Sure, we all love to hear it when our mani or brows are looking immaculate, but compliments about our abilities and skills are the ones that really stick with us. Tell a girl she's hilarious, that she's capable or that her customer service brightened your day, and you'll be contributing to a positive sense of self-worth. What better gift can you give than that?

FACE TIME FOR REAL

Girls need to look out for girls. Sometimes it's the funniest friends, the bossest bitches or the savviest sisters who actually need checking up on. We live in difficult times, and social media makes it easier than ever to wear a mask and pretend everything is OK when really we're falling apart. Make sure you regularly connect with your girl gang IRL as well as through video calls, memes and placing hundreds of flame emojis under each other's selfies on social media. Nothing beats a face-to-face connection for making sure someone's really all right.

All for one

When you already feel like you're spending each day on the warpath in order to get what you want, it can be easy to become insular and forget to look out for the other women around you. A true boss bitch always remembers to pull her girls up behind her. Keep an eye on your fellow workers and advocate for their progress just as hard as you fight for your own. Noticed them killing it in the workplace? Don't just compliment them; drop your boss a line too to say how impressed you've been by their work lately. Powerful women empower other women.

Other women
who are killing it should
motivate you, thrill you,
challenge you
and inspire you.

TAYLOR SWIFT

The union makes us strong

Those three little words every woman needs to hear: join a union. A union's job is to protect employee rights in the workplace, acting as worker representatives during disputes, offering advice and working to improve wages, hours and conditions. Unions have a long history of improving conditions for workers, and they're a great source of support if you encounter problems in your career. They can also connect you with other women in your industry. Want to join a union but don't know where to start? Visit tuc.org.uk in the UK or aflcio.org in the US to learn more.

SISTER-HOOD IS POWER

Stand up to bullies

Sadly, bullying isn't always left behind when we leave high school. Far from being the preserve of the teenage mean girl, the Regina Georges of this world somehow find ways to make themselves known in adulthood and beyond. If you see a bully picking on another person, make your voice heard. Don't let them stand alone. If we don't take the time to stand up when we see wrongs being done, how can we expect others to come to our aid in our own time of need? Look out for your sisters, and they will look out for you.

The success of every woman should be the inspiration to another. We should raise each other up.

SERENA WILLIAMS

CALL OUT
SEXIST ADVERTISING

Picture this: you step onto the train platform waiting to begin your daily commute and looming over you is a 7-ft tall, scantily clad model beside the slogan "Are you bikini body ready?" Chances are this has actually happened to you because this kind of advertising – utilizing harmful stereotypes or weaponizing women's insecurities against them – is still extremely common. But that doesn't mean we have to accept it. Use your voice, queen! Tweet, email, campaign to let the advertisers know that, far from incentivizing you to buy their product, their dinosaur advertising views have made you vow never to shop with them again. Who knows, your angry response could start a movement.

Believe women

Emerging from #MeToo, the social justice movement that sought to empower victims of sexual abuse, these two simple but powerful words – "believe women" – emphasize just how important it is that we accept women's allegations of sex crimes at face value. It fights a historical precedent that views the women who accuse men of sexual abuse as deceptive or vindictive and instead places the emphasis on seeking justice, holding the men who abuse to account.

Some critics are opposed to the "believe women" slogan on the grounds that it assumes the guilt of the male party, but the consequences of not taking this view are too severe to ignore. And it begs the question, when are women's accusations enough to overturn the presumed innocence of one man? With Harvey Weinstein, that number was about 80. With Bill Cosby, it was 60.

Always assuming a man's innocence is to always assume a woman's deceptive nature. This stereotype has caused enormous damage and has destroyed the lives of countless women. It is not tenable. We must believe women, until men abusing their power stops feeling like an inevitability.

I raise up my voice – not so I can shout, but so that those without a voice can be heard.

MALALA YOUSAFZAI

Support women's businesses

Crossing the box in the polling booth on election day isn't the only way you can cast your vote. Voting with your wallet is a powerful way to show society what is important to you and what changes you wish to see. In a world that pays women just 84 per cent of what men make, it is time to put your money back in women's wallets by shopping at female-run businesses. This takes power out of the hands of male-owned businesses that don't necessarily operate with a woman-friendly political agenda in mind and puts it directly into the hands of independent business-owning women. Who knows, you might even find a new favourite product!

GIRLS COMPETE: WOMEN EMPOWER

Invite other women into the conversation

Women belong in all the places where decisions are being made, said the late, great Ruth Bader Ginsburg, former associate justice of the Supreme Court of the USA and all-round badass. If you find yourself in a position to make big decisions, whether at work, in your home life or in a social enterprise, try to resist the urge to believe that your thoughts represent those of all women. Invite other women into the conversation. Consult them, discover their perspectives and try to make choices that speak to a wider women's experience, not just your own. This is the best way to use your platform to advocate for a better future for us all.

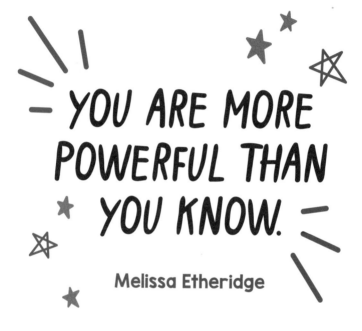

YOU ARE MORE POWERFUL THAN YOU KNOW.

Melissa Etheridge

Be your own role model

Envision the role model you wish your childhood self could have known or seen. What kind of woman would have made little you feel seen, heard, excited and inspired? Be that woman. You may not have had an ideal role model when you were growing up, but that doesn't mean you can't be that woman for another little girl. Consider how your choices may inspire and empower the younger generation. Not only will this give you a new perspective on the person you've become, but it will also inspire you to be the best **you** that you can be.

Be the change you want to see

How many things do we all quietly accept because they're just the way things are? Enough. Life is too short to allow injustices or even annoyances to thrive because we don't think there's any point in fighting them. Just because something has always been that way doesn't mean it has to remain so.

Stand up for what you believe in and have faith in your capacity to make a change. Look to celebrity role models, like singer Billie Eilish whose refusal to wear Oscar de la Renta to the 2021 MET Gala unless the fashion house abandoned fur led to a complete overhaul in their policy. *You* can be the change, so stop leaving it to somebody else.

The more you give, the more you receive

VOLUNTEER!

We are lucky to live in a world with more charities and organizations working to empower women than ever before. And the exciting bit? You can be part of them! Look into volunteering opportunities in your area and see what you can do to empower and enfranchise women across the world. Perhaps that means helping out at your local women's shelter, getting involved in protests for women's rights or taking part in a mentorship scheme. The possibilities are endless.

We need women
at all levels... to make sure
women's voices are
heard and heeded, not
overlooked and ignored.

SHERYL SANDBERG

Is your feminism intersectional?

So, you're a proud, badass feminist. Job done, right? Not quite. If your feminism isn't intersectional, then there's still a long way to go. Intersectional feminism is a version of feminism that fights for the rights of *all* women, taking the vast differences of women's experiences due to sexuality, race, religion and more into consideration. It's the recognition of the way gendered oppression intersects with other kinds of societal oppression. And it's also taking the time to recognize that, while your gender means you suffer various societal oppressions, you may be benefitting from other kinds of privilege – the privilege of being white, straight, cisgender or able-bodied, for example. This does nothing to diminish your experience as a woman; it just means that you may not face double or even triple oppressions in the same way that, say, a transgender Muslim woman may.

Ensuring your feminism and the feminist sources you interact with are as intersectional as possible will help to create a feminist movement and a future society that is more diverse and inclusive for women of all backgrounds and experiences. There are many feminist activists you can look to for insightful explanations of intersectional feminism and how best to practise it, including Kimberlé Crenshaw, Juliet Williams and Roxane Gay.

Say no to slut-shaming

When you grow up in a society that slut-shames women, it's normal for your inner monologue to automatically take part in the conversation. Judging women on how many people they've slept with or for sending nudes is part of an internalized misogyny that almost always accompanies growing up in a sexist society. What you *can* do is call out that bullshit wherever you see it, including in your own attitudes. Stopping slut-shaming means correcting yourself any time you find you're judging a woman for displaying her sexuality or making assumptions about her sexuality based on her appearance. Remind yourself that what a woman chooses to do with her body, in or out of the bedroom, is nobody's business but her own. For more inspiration, check out The UnSlut Project (unslutproject.com) created by Emily Lindin as a safe space to share stories and education around ending slut-shaming for good.

Sisterhood is important because we are all we have to stand on.

Ntozake Shange

Expand your horizons

If we only surround ourselves with women who look and think like us, our world view will never expand beyond very narrow horizons. If you want to see the bigger picture and create real, positive change in the world, then you need to start meeting people who are nothing like you. Seek out friendships with women from different walks of life and you'll be amazed, not only by how much fun you can have with women who differ from you, but also by how dramatically it expands your world view.

Let your light
help others'
shine brighter

Check your privilege

Having privilege means that you have certain advantages in society, usually based on factors outside of your control such as race, gender or sexuality. Privilege is a nuanced concept, and you can be both oppressed by and benefited by society for different reasons. For example, you may be a lesbian woman who is affected by homophobia but also be cisgender (meaning you identify as the gender you were assigned at birth). To say that you're privileged isn't to suggest that your life has been free from struggle. Acknowledging your privilege and the ways it benefits you, such as offering you more opportunities or shielding you from prejudice is a key step in developing your feminism, empathizing with others and using that privilege to advocate, knowing when to speak up and when to let others lead.

For some reason,
I have better luck when
I work with women. I
guess I have a good
sense of sisterhood.

DOLLY PARTON

Build your sisters up

If gossipy tabloids are your guilty pleasure, then you're no stranger to the "sidebar of shame", a fuzzy photo of a celebrity with (gasp) *cellulite* – or, heaven forbid – *a little belly*, turned into a fully-fledged "article" highlighting exactly what is "wrong" with her. Or perhaps simply all signs that she might actually be enjoying her body without factoring in the paparazzi hiding in the bushes.

When we grow up in this culture of shame, it's easy for these views of other women to have leaked into our subconscious. But if the film *Mean Girls* has taught us anything, it's that tearing down other women won't make you feel any stronger. Look on other women's "flaws" with kindness and say "fuck you" to that inner voice that feels a little smug when your colleague gains some weight, or your neighbour takes her bins out in Crocs. If we're kinder to the women around us, we might just start being kinder to ourselves.

FEMINISM IS A VERB

Feminism is more than a state of mind. It's a verb. This means that to call yourself a feminist in the truest sense of the word, you need to be actively performing feminism in your day-to-day life. Don't let this daunt you; it's empowering! It means getting out in the world and challenging the sexist bullshit it throws at you. It means supporting your sisters in their time of need. It means taking on all the shitty, misogynistic crap we are expected to put up with and saying: "No, actually. I don't think so." So, don't just *be* a feminist. Go forth and *do* feminism.

Know when to say you fucked up

Every badass woman knows when to admit she's messed up. Making mistakes is part of being human – it's how you respond to those mistakes that define who you are. When somebody calls you out for your actions, or something you've said, make sure that you've really *heard* what they're trying to say. Often our reflex, when criticized, is to rush to defend ourselves, but launching into an immediate response can mean we don't take the time to properly understand what the person criticizing us is trying to say. This leaves no room for growth.

Making a mistake doesn't mean you're a bad person, and it doesn't mean the person calling you out thinks you're a bad person either. Taking the time to tell you that you got it wrong means they see the potential for you to change.

Next time somebody calls you out, take time to pause. If you need to process their comments, that's OK. Tell them you will sit with their words and come back to them when you've fully thought about what they've said. Then formulate a response that not only accounts for their feelings but offers practical steps to show you will do better next time. Remember, it's always OK to fuck up. It's what you do next that shows who you are.

The way to achieve your own success is to be willing to help somebody else get it first.

IYANLA VANZANT

Know how to say someone else fucked up

Part of being a badass woman is using your voice to call people out when they mess up. But this isn't about point scoring or superiority; it's about using your own voice to offer people a chance to grow. There's an art to telling somebody, "Hey, you messed up." Follow these steps to call somebody out productively.

1. Wait until your anger has subsided.

2. Make it clear that your issue is with their behaviour, not with them. This is especially important when talking to a friend. Rather than launch accusations at their character, talk about why their actions or their language is inappropriate.

Know your boundaries and what kinds of apologies just won't cut it. Part of being a badass is knowing when to let toxic people go.

Fill your life with badass women

Your sisters are your soulmates

Put your friends first. There's an iconic scene in *Sex and the City* where, amid all the boy-chasing, sexual escapades and jaw-dropping fits, Charlotte looks at the girls with whom she's shared her prime years in New York City, and says, "Don't laugh at me, but maybe we could be each other's soulmates. And then we could let men be just these great, nice guys to have fun with." Let this be your mantra. Through thick and thin, your girls will have your back. Invest in them. Be there for them. Hold each other's hands through the highs and the lows. Your friendships with your girls will be the most loving relationships of your life. Cherish them.

Conclusion

Find the nearest mirror, take a long hard look at yourself and smile. That's a badass staring back at you. In finishing this book, you've equipped yourself to do battle with society's expectations of womanhood. No more will you shrink yourself to be accepted, but you'll stand tall, shout loud and make your thoughts and feelings known.

You are ready to give yourself full permission to live exactly how you want, wear what you want, do what you want and spend time with people who make you feel seen and loved. No more asking for permission to live your best life because now you know that there's nothing more badass than being your full self, without apology.

When I'm hungry, I eat. When I'm thirsty, I drink. When I feel like saying something, I say it.

MADONNA

Have you enjoyed this book? If so, find us on
Facebook at **Summersdale Publishers**,
on Twitter at **@Summersdale** and on
Instagram at **@summersdalebooks** and
get in touch. We'd love to hear from you!

www.summersdale.com